DIOSA

Edwin Sánchez

BROADWAY PLAY PUBLISHING INC
New York
www.broadwayplaypublishing.com
info@broadwayplaypublishing.com

First printing December 2011
I S B N: 978-0-88145-497-0

Book design: Marie Donovan
Page make-up: Adobe Indesign
Typeface: Palatino
Printed and bound in the U S A

ABOUT THE AUTHOR

Recent productions include TRAFFICKING IN
BROKEN HEARTS at the Celebration Theater in Los
Angeles as well as the world premiere of his romantic
comedy I'LL TAKE ROMANCE at the Evolution
Theater in Ohio. His newest play LA BELLA FAMILIA
will be produced by Teatro Vista in Chicago in
2011. Other productions include, DIOSA, produced
by Hartford Stage after a successful workshop
by New York Stage and Film, TRAFFICKING IN
BROKEN HEARTS at the Atlantic Theater in New
York, UNMERCIFUL GOOD FORTUNE at the Intar
Theater in New York, ICARUS produced by Fourth
Unity in New York, Actors Theater of Louisville as
part of their Humana Festival, and San Jose Rep in
California. His play BAREFOOT BOY WITH SHOES
ON was produced by Primary Stages in New York
and was selected by the Eugene O'Neill Playwrights
Conference to represent the National Playwrights
Conference at the Schelykovo Playwrights Seminar
in Russia. Mr Sánchez' work has been produced
regionally throughout the United States as well as
Brazil and Switzerland. Among his awards are the
Kennedy Center Fund for New American Plays
(CLEAN), three New York Foundation for the Arts
Playwriting/Screenwriting Fellowships, the Princess
Grace Playwriting Fellowship (UNMERCIFUL
GOOD FORTUNE), the Daryl Roth Creative Spirit

Award and the A T & T On Stage New Play Award
(UNMERCIFUL GOOD FORTUNE). Mr Sánchez lives
in upstate New York where he continues to write as
well as teach and mentors playwrights.

DIOSA was first produced by Hartford Stage, running from 10 April-11 May 2003. The cast and creative contributors were:

JOSEFA ....Karina Michaels
MIGUEL ....Robert Montano
AMBER ....Josie de Guzman
KRAMER..Edmond Genest
CHRIS ....Matthew Mabe
STEWART...Roderick Hill

Director .... Melia Bensussen
Costume design ....Catherine Zuber
Set design ....Christine Jones
Lighting design ....Robert Wierzel
Sound design...David Van Tieghem
Choreography ....Willie Rosario

CAST OF CHARACTERS

JOSEFA, *ages from 15 to 22. The unambitious girl who discovers in dance both a prison and a means to escape.*

MIGUEL, JOSEFA's *father. Obsessed with stardom, he is willing to do anything for success.*

AMBER, JOSEFA's *mother. Older than her husband,* MIGUEL, *and actually a wonderful dancer in her own right, she is blindly devoted to* MIGUEL *and to keeping him.*

CHRIS, a *small time player in the studio system, he discovers* JOSEFA *and as much as he sees her as a meal ticket there is a part of him that loves her.*

KRAMER, *the studio head who signs* MIGUEL, *and as an afterthought,* Josefa, *only to fire her when she defies him.*

STEWART, *the lowest man on the studio totem pole, but the one who provides* JOSEFA *with the necessary info to trump* KRAMER *and start her journey to the top.*

ACT ONE

(From the darkness hand claps begin. The sound of someone keeping rhythm.)

MIGUEL: *(V O)* Again *(More hand claps)* Again!

(Lights slowly up on the front porch of the TORRES family home. MIGUEL is trying to teach his daughter, JOSEFA, how to dance. He is 32, attractive and neatly dressed. She is 15 and slightly overweight.)

MIGUEL: *Niña! Niña estupida.* You don't want to learn.

JOSEFA: No, I do

MIGUEL: You're a stick. It's like dancing with a piece of wood.

JOSEFA: really I do. I swear I want to.

MIGUEL: *(Softens, touches her hair) Niña...Niña estupida.*

JOSEFA: I'm sorry.

MIGUEL: Come on, let's do it again.

(MIGUEL holds out his hand to JOSEFA, she takes it while staring at his feet.)

MIGUEL: Am I down there?

JOSEFA: Your feet are.

MIGUEL: Look up at me. All dancing is done with the eyes.
Good dancing anyway. Remember that.

(JOSEFA *looks up at* MIGUEL. *They begin to dance, she stumbles.*)

MIGUEL: You're useless. (*He strikes a dance pose and holds it.*) You see this? This is gonna get me what I want.

AMBER: (*V O*) Josefa! Josefa, come help mami pick her perfume.

MIGUEL: Go ahead, *niña estupida*. Why do you always disappoint me?

JOSEFA: I'm sorry.

(MIGUEL *ignores her and continues dancing by himself on the porch.* JOSEFA *enters the house. Through a scrim we see* AMBER, *her mother, as she sits in front of a mirror at her dressing table.* AMBER *retouches her already slightly over made up face.*)

AMBER: Baby, pick *mami*'s perfume. Are you crying?

JOSEFA: (*Hiding her face*) No.

AMBER: Baby, never ever cry in front of a man. It does no good.

JOSEFA: He's not a man, he's my father.

AMBER: You're fifteen. He's a man.

JOSEFA: (*Softly*) He's supposed to be my *papi*.

AMBER: Pick something for Mami. Something romantic.

(JOSEFA *begins to look through the perfume as* AMBER *applies the finishing touches to herself. She takes a sip from her ever present teacup.*)

AMBER: Men don't believe in tears.

JOSEFA: What do they believe in?

(JOSEFA *hands* AMBER *the perfume she has picked for her.*)

AMBER: Sweet things. Men like sweet things.

MIGUEL: (*Calling her from other room.*) Amber.

JOSEFA: What do woman like?

AMBER: It doesn't matter. Josefa, expect nothing and life will be wonderful.

JOSEFA: You look pretty, Mami.

AMBER: *(Correcting her)* Uh uh.

JOSEFA: You look beautiful, Mami.

AMBER: Ah, that's better.

(AMBER rises. She is wearing a lovely long dress. JOSEFA sprays her with perfume as AMBER checks herself one last time in the mirror and joins MIGUEL in his dance. They fit perfectly into each other. They continue to dance as he gives his final orders to JOSEFA.)

MIGUEL: Now you lock up and don't open the door to anyone after we leave.

JOSEFA: Yes, Papi.

MIGUEL: And wash and starch my dance shirts.

JOSEFA: Yes, Papi.

MIGUEL: And be in bed by the time we get home.

JOSEFA: Yes, Papi.

(MIGUEL dips AMBER in a low, seductive way. She caresses his face, he stares at her. She is about to kiss him.)

MIGUEL: You need more makeup.

AMBER: Yes Papi, uh, Miguel. ...I thought I was fine.

(AMBER exits back to her makeup table. JOSEFA notices her mother's embarrassment.)

MIGUEL: Hollywood people will be there, you never know. They come to drink but there's no reason they can't discover a bright new star. Someone to make women all over America swoon.

JOSEFA: She looked beautiful.

MIGUEL: What did you say?

JOSEFA: Nothing.

MIGUEL: Stop mumbling.

(JOSEFA *points to the back of her head.*)

MIGUEL: What's the matter with you?

JOSEFA: I can see your bald spot, Papi.

(MIGUEL *slaps* JOSEFA's *hand away, rearranges his hair.*)

MIGUEL: I parted my hair wrong, that's all. *Niña estupida. (To* AMBER*)* Are you ready?

AMBER: *(Hurrying in)* Yes, yes.

MIGUEL: How do I look?

AMBER: Wonderful, Miguel. Perfect.

(MIGUEL *kisses* AMBER's *hand.*)

AMBER: And me?

MIGUEL: Get your wrap, come on. *(He studies her face for a moment.)* You can finish putting your makeup on in the car.

JOSEFA: Good-bye, Mami. You look beautiful.

(AMBER *and* MIGUEL *exit to the small club where they perform.*)

VOICE: Ladies and gentlemen, here they are, the love birds of dance, please welcome, Miguel and Amber.

(MIGUEL *takes center stage and holds out his hand to* AMBER, *who circles him and joins him. They begin to dance. From her room,* JOSEFA *begins to dance. Whereas before she was stiff, without her father she moves gracefully, matching her mother's movements perfectly.* MIGUEL *and* AMBER *finish their dance and bow to a smattering of applause.* JOSEFA *also bows. She looks at herself in the mirror. She puts a small dab of her mother's perfume behind her ears.*)

JOSEFA: *Niña estupida.*

(The music begins again for another dance for MIGUEL *and* AMBER. *They bow and begin to dance again as lights fade on them.* JOSEFA *looks at herself in the mirror. Her parents argue off stage.* JOSEFA *sets up an ironing board and gets a basket of her father's unironed shirts.)*

AMBER: *(V O)* One man said it, Miguel. One! An ugly, old fat man.

*(*AMBER *and* MIGUEL *enter the house and go past* JOSEFA, *who is now ironing, into their bedroom.)*

MIGUEL: Who could have been a studio executive for all you know.

AMBER: So? He wouldn't be the only one in Hollywood.

MIGUEL: Amber, if one person says it a hundred thought it but didn't have the—

AMBER: Bad taste.

MIGUEL: —nerve to say it.

AMBER: Nerve? To insult your wife?

MIGUEL: That's the problem. They don't think of you as my wife. Sweetheart, he asked me if you were my mother.

*(*JOSEFA *notices she has almost burnt her father's shirt by eavesdropping. She moves the iron and checks the shirt to make sure there is no damage to it.)*

AMBER: What? What do you want me to do, Miguel? Tell me. I'll do it. I can dye my hair, change my dress. What?

*(*MIGUEL *begins to gently kiss* AMBER's *shoulders.)*

MIGUEL: You know I will always think you're beautiful.

AMBER: Miguel, stop it.

*(*MIGUEL *kisses* AMBER's *neck.)*

MIGUEL: All the time it takes you to get ready, you can't enjoy that.

AMBER: Miguel, I don't mind. Really.

MIGUEL: Ssshh. I need someone younger. Just for the act, that's all. ...Josefa's going to have to dance with me.

AMBER: No.

MIGUEL: Ambersita.

AMBER: She can't dance.

MIGUEL: She can and she will. We've been teaching her all her life. She's lazy. You spoil her.

(JOSEFA *very deliberately puts the iron back on* MIGUEL*'s white dress shirt. She removes her hand from the iron, letting it char the shirt.*)

AMBER: She's just a girl.

MIGUEL: Exactly. A young girl. We look closer in age than you and I do.

(AMBER *stalks into the room where* JOSEFA *is ironing. They stare at each other.*)

MIGUEL: *(Calling after her as he enters.)* Amber.

(MIGUEL *sees the smoke coming from his shirt.*)

MIGUEL: My shirt! What have you done?!

(MIGUEL *takes the iron off the shirt, the shirt is ruined. He turns to face* JOSEFA *still holding the hot iron in his hand.*)

MIGUEL: *Niña estupida!*

AMBER: Miguel! Let me talk to Josefa. Alone. Please Miguel.

(AMBER *pulls* JOSEFA *towards her dressing table.*)

JOSEFA: I'm not gonna dance with you.

MIGUEL: Yes you will.

AMBER: Miguel, be quiet. Just leave us alone. *Por favor.*

(MIGUEL *storms off with his charred shirt.* AMBER *and* JOSEFA *stand in front of* AMBER's *mirror.)*

JOSEFA: Look, *mami,* we could be sisters.

(AMBER *kisses* JOSEFA, *then sits in front of the mirror. She begins to take off her makeup.)*

JOSEFA: Mami, don't.

AMBER: Have you ever seen me without my makeup? Even in the morning? Do you know how much older I am than your father?

(JOSEFA *shakes her head no.)*

AMBER: I hope you never fall in love, Josefa. It sounds like a terrible thing to say, but it's not. Your father was a boy when I met him. A beautiful, ambitious, sexy boy. He's still a boy. My boy. When your father first saw me he ran out and bought dozens of caramels. He said that was my coloring, sweet caramel. He ate them all in one sitting and got so sick. He proposed the next day, and every day after until I said yes. He chased me until I caught him. If you don't do this for me, Josefa, he's gonna get somebody else. Somebody I can't trust. And that will kill me. Help me. Help me hold on to him. He asks so little. Just dance with him, that's all.

JOSEFA: But I can't dance.

AMBER: Sssh. I know you dance by yourself. When you think no one can see you. Josefa, I'm your mother. You'll never be able to keep a secret from me. *(Her face is bare of all makeup.)*

JOSEFA: Mami, I've never seen you without makeup.

AMBER: And it was always my plan that you never would. I fought a good fight but time won. It always does.

(AMBER *laughs to herself, kisses the top of* JOSEFA*'s head.*
Amber rises from her seat and cedes it to JOSEFA, *who*
reluctantly sits.)

JOSEFA: I'm not beautiful like you, Mami.

AMBER: No. You're not. Thank goodness.

(AMBER *applies a small but perfect amount of makeup to*
JOSEFA*'s face.)*

AMBER: You're so young. You don't need much make
up. Now don't cry.

JOSEFA: Okay, Mami.

AMBER: Be pretty. Yes? Just make daddy happy.

JOSEFA: Will it make you happy, Mami?

AMBER: Yes.

JOSEFA: 'kay.

(AMBER *begins to brush* JOSEFA*'s hair. Lights up to dim on*
MIGUEL *as he dances by himself. He repeats a move over*
and over again. AMBER *exits.* JOSEFA *rises from the dressing*
table and steps out of her dress. Her pink full slip should be
padded to make her appear thick waisted. She stands, barely
seen in the shadows, watching her father dance. AMBER
enters carrying the dress she had been wearing. AMBER
helps her into her dress which barely fits the plumper
JOSEFA. *Amber takes the flower from behind her ear and pins*
it in JOSEFA*'s hair. She holds her hand for a beat and exits.*
MIGUEL *turns and catches* JOSEFA *staring at him, he smiles.*
JOSEFA *repeats* MIGUEL*'s step.)*

MIGUEL: Again.

(JOSEFA *comes closer and tries again.)*

MIGUEL: Again!

(JOSEFA *comes closer and tries again.)*

MIGUEL: *Niña estupida!* Again!

(Bolero music is heard.)

VOICE: ...the love birds of dance, please welcome, Miguel and Amber.

(MIGUEL enters, holds out his hand and JOSEFA enters. While JOSEFA is nervous at first, when she finally looks at the audience she is transformed, dancing full out. She and her father dance. For the first time it is not about playing to the audience for MIGUEL, but about this "woman" in his arms. It's as if he were discovering the romance of dance for the very first time. At the end of the dance they strike the same romantic pose as AMBER and MIGUEL. They enter their dressing room. He tries not to look at her.)

MIGUEL: You weren't bad out there. One or two things that we need to look at, but... *(Noticing her stillness)* You weren't nervous at all, were you?

JOSEFA: A little bit.

MIGUEL: No, you weren't.

JOSEFA: No, I wasn't.

(JOSEFA sits in front of her mirror and is about to take off her makeup.)

MIGUEL: No. Don't. Don't take it off. You look so grown up. *(He points to her reflection.)* Look who's pretty tonight.

(A knock is heard on the door)

MIGUEL: *(To door)* My wife is changing, we'll be right out. *(To JOSEFA)* It's much too late to drive back across the border. Why don't we stay in town tonight? *(He takes the rose from behind her ear, he pulls off the petals and lets them rain on her.)* And tomorrow we get you your own dress. The most beautiful dress we can find. You shouldn't have to wear your mother's hand me downs anymore.

JOSEFA: I don't mind. ...Papi. Mami's better. A better dancer.

(MIGUEL *turns to face* JOSEFA.)

MIGUEL: That'll change.

JOSEFA: *(Almost whispered.)* ...I love dancing with you.

(Song: I'm Gonna Buy a Paper Doll *begins to play, lights out on them up as he gently carries her into the shadows, her head resting on his shoulder. Lights up on* AMBER *ironing. The lights come up behind her to reveal row upon row of starched and ironed white dress shirts. The glamorous and over made up woman we saw at the beginning is no more. She is not slovenly, just plain. She pulls out another shirt to iron but instead she has pulled out* JOSEFA'*s pink slip. There is a red stain on the front of it.* AMBER *looks at it for a moment then balls it up, putting it back in the basket and pulling out another of* MIGUEL'*s shirts. A faint applause is heard. She smiles, acknowledges the applause as if it were for her.)*

(Lights out on her and up on MIGUEL *and* JOSEFA *as they finish their dance. A year has passed.* JOSEFA *is now sixteen. Her body has changed. She is slimmer and more womanly than before. Their new costumes reflect an upturn in their fortunes since* MIGUEL *added* JOSEFA *to the act. As they bow,* CHRIS *enters and proffers his business card. He is in is late twenties.* MIGUEL *stops* JOSEFA.*)*

CHRIS: Chris Malloy, Empire Pictures. Can I talk to you, Mister Torres, can I call you Miguel? I just wanted to tell you how impressed I was with your little act here. Won't you please join me? Ah, both of you, of course.

JOSEFA: I'm going to the dressing room.

MIGUEL: She's a little shy. *(Hard, to* JOSEFA*)* Don't embarrass me.

CHRIS: Actually, Miguel, you're the one I'm really interested in talking to. There's no need for your wife, I'm sorry, I forgot her name, to be here.

(JOSEFA *goes off to their dressing room.*)

CHRIS: Miguel, you are leading man material. You have that stardom glow.

MIGUEL: I always thought I did.

CHRIS: And you were right. All you need is a screen test to prove it.

MIGUEL: And you can get me that?

(CHRIS *smiles and takes a sip of his drink.*)

CHRIS: It all depends on how much you want it.

MIGUEL: More than anything. It's my dream.

CHRIS: You're already such a lucky man, Miguel. Talented, good looking and with such an attractive young wife.

(MIGUEL *is silent.*)

CHRIS: Perhaps I could tell her just how pretty she is? (*He offers his hand.*) And how famous her husband is going to be.

(MIGUEL *doesn't move.*)

CHRIS: Or was I wrong about you?

(MIGUEL *takes his hand, shakes it.*)

(JOSEFA *sits in front of the makeup table in the dressing room. A knock is heard,* CHRIS *enters. An other worldly version of* Paper Doll *begins to play. Lights go down on dressing room. Lights shift to* MIGUEL *knocking on the dressing room door.*)

MIGUEL: Josefa.

(Lights come back up on dressing room. JOSEFA sits on the floor, her dress half on and half off. CHRIS is buckling his pants.)

MIGUEL: Josefa.

CHRIS: Answer him.

JOSEFA: Yes, Papi. I'll be right out.

CHRIS: Papi? I knew you couldn't be his wife. You're a real good daughter though, you got him a screen test.

(CHRIS offers his hand to help JOSEFA stand, she hesitates then takes it.)

JOSEFA: Can my mother be in the test with him?

CHRIS: Not you?

(JOSEFA shakes her head.)

CHRIS: You're awfully pretty.

JOSEFA: My mother's prettier. She's really beautiful.

CHRIS: Okay. I'll see what I can do.

JOSEFA: You're a big shot, right?

MIGUEL: *(V O)* Josefa!

CHRIS: Right. *(He heads to the door, stops.)* You know, when you were dancing I couldn't take my eyes off you.

(CHRIS exits. MIGUEL enters. Silence)

MIGUEL: He, he wanted to congratulate you, he told me. ...You hungry? You should eat. Maybe you should eat.

(MIGUEL holds up her coat, she puts it on. He exits as MAKE-UP MAN enters. They are now at Empire Film Studio.)

MAKE-UP MAN: Next! Amber Torres.

JOSEFA: I'll go get her.

MAKE-UP MAN: Tell her it's make-up first, then hair, then straight to the set. You got that?

JOSEFA: Yes, sir.

(JOSEFA *finds her parents.* MIGUEL *is kneeling in prayer,* AMBER *stands over him, combing his hair.* JOSEFA *watches them, they don't see her.* MIGUEL *finishes praying and crosses himself.* AMBER *tries to help him stand.)*

MIGUEL: I can stand up by myself.

AMBER: I know you can.

MIGUEL: I'm not nervous you know.

AMBER: Why should you be? You're going to amaze them.

MIGUEL: You think so, right?

AMBER: Of course.

MIGUEL: You should put on some makeup or something.

AMBER: They said they would call me when they were ready for me.

MIGUEL: You won't let me fail, right Amber?

(AMBER *kisses* MIGUEL *on the cheek.)*

MIGUEL: The makeup!

AMBER: I'm sorry.

MIGUEL: It's just that...I look okay, right? Perfect?

(AMBER *nods, turns away,* MIGUEL *grabs her hand, kisses it and holds it to his heart. He begins to cry softly.)*

AMBER: Ssshh, Miguel. I'm here. Where I'll always be.

(MIGUEL *shakes his head, breathes and calms himself.* JOSEFA *enters.)*

MIGUEL: I've waited my whole life for this. For this one moment.

JOSEFA: They're ready for you, mami.

MIGUEL: Amber. Her name is Amber, and my name is Miguel. We are Miguel and Amber, the love birds of dance. We are not your parents today.

(JOSEFA *nods.* AMBER *breaks away from* MIGUEL, *who starts practicing a few of his steps and follows* JOSEFA *towards makeup.* JOSEFA *steals another looks at* MIGUEL, *so does* AMBER.)

AMBER: He didn't mean that.

JOSEFA: It doesn't matter.

AMBER: He's just so nervous. …What if I ruin this for him?

JOSEFA: Don't say that. You won't.

AMBER: Everybody in his family was a dancer. Look how far he's come.

JOSEFA: Good for him.

AMBER: No, good for us. We're a family. When he gets his contract everything will change for us, you'll see. You'll go back to school.

JOSEFA: I'm too old for school.

AMBER: You're sixteen.

JOSEFA: Yeah, I can be the oldest girl in the fourth grade.

AMBER: …And…we'll get a house, a nice one. And I'll give you back everything you lost. I swear it. Do you love me, Josefa?

JOSEFA: Yes, of course, Mami.

AMBER: Then you love him. Because I love him. With all my stupid heart.

(AMBER *sinks to the ground,* JOSEFA *tries to help her up.*)

AMBER: I can't. I can't do this.

JOSEFA: Mami, get up, come on. They're waiting for you.

AMBER: I can't, I can't do it.

(AMBER *takes out her flask and tries to drink from it,* JOSEFA *wrests it from her.*)

JOSEFA: Mami, he's waiting for you. Just stand up. Come on.

AMBER: *(Sweetly) Niña estupida.* Help him.

JOSEFA: No. He can dance alone.

AMBER: Please. If I ruin this for him, he'll never forgive me. With you he has a chance. The act was never a success with me, but with you, you brought him luck. Please. It has to be you. Do this for him. Please. Do it for me.

JOSEFA: No. I will not feel sorry for him.

(*Lights out on* JOSEFA *and* AMBER. *Lights up on* MIGUEL.)

ASSISTANT: Miguel Torres test. Rolling.

(MIGUEL *dances by himself for a bit, he gets to center, holds out his hand, nothing and then* JOSEFA *appears in her mother's place.* MIGUEL *barely reacts to the change. Everything about* JOSEFA's *dancing is about making* MIGUEL *look good. Lights continue on them as they dance and come up on* CHRIS, KRAMER *and* STUART *as they watch the screen test.*)

CHRIS: Latin lover. Can play the swarthy type. We always need some color for the background.

KRAMER: Yeah, okay, six months.

(MIGUEL *and* JOSEFA *separate, but continue dancing. Lights dim on him but stay bright on her. They all watch her.*)

KRAMER: And who's this? His wife?

CHRIS: Uh, daughter, I think.

KRAMER: Peaches and cream. She a minor?

CHRIS: Yeah.

KRAMER: You sleep with her?

CHRIS: Of course not.

KRAMER: Uh huh.

CHRIS: Hey, gimme a break, her father was with us the entire time.

KRAMER: What does that mean? No?

(MIGUEL *and* JOSEFA *finish their dance.* MIGUEL *looks straight ahead, as if into a camera. Lights come up to bright on him and dim on* JOSEFA.)

STUART: Name.

MIGUEL: Miguel Torres, but I'm willing to change it.

STUART: Please turn left, right and back to center. Thank you.

(MIGUEL *nods, smiles, turns to the left, then right profile and back to the center. As the lights on him are dimming a faint light is on* JOSEFA, *staring at her father.* KRAMER *and* STUART *start to exit.*)

KRAMER: Oh, and uh ...

STUART: Stuart.

KRAMER: Yeah, Stewie. Sign the girl, too.

STUART: Check.

(Pop. *the sound of a champagne bottle being uncorked. It is a party for* MIGUEL. AMBER *is pouring champagne. Chris accepts some champagne from* AMBER. JOSEFA *stands off to the side;* AMBER *approaches her, offering her a glass.*)

AMBER: I guess it's okay for my little girl to join us in a toast tonight.

(JOSEFA *takes the glass.*)

AMBER: You did good. Thank you so much. *(She kisses* JOSEFA.*)* Attention, everybody, I want to propose a toast. First, I want to thank our honored guest Christopher for joining us tonight...

(CHRIS *nods his head uncomfortably. He and* MIGUEL *lock eyes for a beat.)*

AMBER: And to Miguel, my most wonderful, and soon to be a big star, husband. Congratulations, *mi amor.*

(AMBER *and* MIGUEL *kiss.)*

AMBER: And let's not forget the little girl who made it all possible—

MIGUEL: *(Cutting her off)* Dance with me, Ambersita.

(MIGUEL *pulls* AMBER *to his side and they begin to dance.* JOSEFA *exits to the porch, the music is fainter now. She takes some cigarettes from a hiding place, lights one and inhales deeply. Unseen by her,* CHRIS *follows her out.* JOSEFA *tastes the champagne, makes a face and pours it out.)*

CHRIS: It's pretty bad, isn't it?

(JOSEFA *is about to get rid of her cigarette.)*

CHRIS: Oh, don't mind me. Got another cigarette?

JOSEFA: *(Lying, hiding her pack of cigarettes)* No.

(CHRIS *pours out his champagne.)*

CHRIS: It taste like piss.

JOSEFA: Have you had piss? *(Silence)* My mother got the best one she could.

CHRIS: You'd think she'd know a little more about alcohol, wouldn't you?

(JOSEFA *turns to exit.)*

CHRIS: You still haven't said thank you.

JOSEFA: Thank you.

CHRIS: You don't even know why you're saying it, do you?

JOSEFA: You asked me to say thank you so I said thank you.

CHRIS: Most girls would be grateful for a studio contract.

JOSEFA: It should have been my mother.

CHRIS: So turn it down.

JOSEFA: I can't. My father said he's gonna use the money to get a new car.

CHRIS: Wait a second. Your money? He's gonna use your money?

JOSEFA: It's the family's money.

CHRIS: Uh huh. (*He looks in on* AMBER *and* MIGUEL *dancing.*) He's very good. He teach you?

JOSEFA: Yeah.

CHRIS: I could tell, cause you're very good.

JOSEFA: No I'm not.

CHRIS: Yes you are. Really. I can't dance. At all. I got two left feet, so I admire anybody who can.

JOSEFA: Anybody can dance.

CHRIS: Oh yeah? Okay, dance with me.

JOSEFA: No.

CHRIS: Pleeease.

JOSEFA: (*Laughs, in spite of herself*) No. No thank you.

(CHRIS *slowly approaches* JOSEFA. *She holds up her cigarette to ward him off.*)

CHRIS: Please Joe-see-fa, dance with me.

JOSEFA: (*Playfully*) I won't dance with any man who can't pronounce my name.

CHRIS: No, but you'll let them fuck you. *(Silence)* I'm sorry.

(JOSEFA goes past him into the house, he tries to stop her, she burns him with her cigarette. In the house MIGUEL and AMBER strike the final pose of their dance. MIGUEL and JOSEFA lock eyes. CHRIS enters behind JOSEFA. JOSEFA storms off into her room. After a beat MIGUEL follows her. AMBER is momentarily left alone. She sees CHRIS, holds out her arms to him.)

AMBER: Come on. Dance with me.

CHRIS: I don't dance.

(CHRIS doesn't get to finish as AMBER leads him in dance. He can't dance.)

AMBER: Someday you're going to be known as the man who discovered Miguel Torres.

CHRIS: You're too kind.

AMBER: And you're so graceful.

CHRIS: No, I'm not.

AMBER: And modest. That such an important man could be so modest.

CHRIS: Maybe we can sit this dance out.

AMBER: I'm boring you.

CHRIS: Oh no, of course not.

AMBER: Men are so much more interesting than women, what could I possibly have to say to you?

CHRIS: Maybe we could have some more of that wonderful champagne.

(AMBER stops, smiles.)

AMBER: I wanted to thank you for taking Josefa.

CHRIS: I beg your pardon?

AMBER: I know you must be surrounded by really beautiful women all the time, so thank you for taking on Josefa.

CHRIS: Josefa's very pretty.

AMBER: You're such a gentleman. Most people think we're sisters.

CHRIS: I never even would have guessed that you were her mother.

AMBER: *(Laughs)* That's because I'm the color of coffee and milk and Josefa's just the color of milk. Such a silly, pretty little girl. Perhaps you'd like to call on her?

CHRIS: Oh, uh, sure, now, weren't we on our way to get some more champagne?

AMBER: Oh, I don't think I should have anymore. Two's my limit.

CHRIS: You've had three.

AMBER: You naughty boy. Buy why shouldn't I, my husband's about to become Hollywood's latest leading man.

(Lights slowly fade on AMBER and CHRIS as she continues to lead him in dance. Light up on a film set.)

STUART: Quiet please. "Jitterbug Commanche On the Warpath". Take one, scene forty nine. Camera rolling, action.

(Tribal drums. A bare chested MIGUEL appears in indian war paint, he scans the horizon, tomahawk in midair. He and JOSEFA, with a papoose on her back, do a jitterbug to Commanche War Dance, *the number should be ridiculous and over the top, but he takes it seriously, emoting and upstaging his daughter at every turn. A shot is heard, he clutches his heart and dies very dramatically. JOSEFA, the Indian maiden, looks at his fallen body and screams [badly].)*

VOICE: *(Continuing)* Cut. The scream is terrible.

(STUART *enters.*)

STUART: Scream is terrible.

VOICE: And could the Indian just die please?

STUART: *(Loudly)* Just die, Indian.

(MIGUEL *jumps up, he is immediately apologetic, while* JOSEFA *goes back to her original place.*)

MIGUEL: You're the boss, sir. I'm willing to stay here all [night if need be.]

VOICE: *(Cutting him off)* We're hoping it won't be quite that long. Let's do a pick up just before the gun shot. Slate it.

STUART: *Apache Hills.* Take two, scene forty nine. Camera rolling, action.

(MIGUEL *does his bit, this time he falls over, seemingly at random.*)

VOICE: Christ, did the Indian just trip?

MIGUEL: No, well, you said [just to die].

STUART: Keep going.

(JOSEFA *enters, having just witnessed* MIGUEL's *fall, she is actually laughing instead of screaming. She covers her mouth to hide her laugh.*)

VOICE: Cut. That was it. Just cut from him earlier to her, that's all. Good scream. Indian one, dismissed, maiden, back tomorrow.

STUART: Good scream.

JOSEFA: *(To no one in particular)* It wasn't even a scream.

STUART: Everybody, let's set up for the next one.

(STUART *exits.* JOSEFA *offers to help* MIGUEL *up, he slaps her hand away.*)

MIGUEL: You got fifteen minutes, fifteen, to be in the parking lot.

(MIGUEL *storms out as* CHRIS *enters.*)

CHRIS: That wasn't a scream.

(JOSEFA *turns to leave.*)

You were laughing at him.

JOSEFA: No, actually I was laughing at us.

CHRIS: Do you two always work together?

JOSEFA: No, sometimes he gets to be an idiot all by himself. ...But he likes it. He really does.

CHRIS: And you?

JOSEFA: Whenever they really let us dance. That's nice. I like that.

CHRIS: How about dinner?

JOSEFA: Are they ever gonna give him a chance to show what he can do? A real part or something?

CHRIS: How about dinner?

(JOSEFA *shakes her head.*)

JOSEFA: No. No thank you.

CHRIS: Well, let me drive you home. We need to talk.

JOSEFA: No we [don't].

CHRIS: (*Cutting her off*) They're dropping your father's option. We're keeping yours. Hey, a pretty girl is never a liability.

JOSEFA: He's the one who wants it.

CHRIS: That's life.

JOSEFA: If he goes I go.

CHRIS: Fine. Plenty of other pretty girls out there. Just like you.

JOSEFA: No. Not just like me.

(JOSEFA *grabs his face in her hands and kisses him, hard. She walks out.*)

CHRIS: Hey! You bit me!

(*Lights up on porch.* AMBER *is massaging* MIGUEL's *neck.*)

MIGUEL: She's not doing anything to help me. To help the family. She should be telling everybody that they're wasting me.

AMBER: Who can she tell?

MIGUEL: Men look at her. Smile at her. It wouldn't kill her to smile back. (*He kisses* AMBER's *hand.*) Women, especially young women, can do things for men that they can't do for themselves. You know that. Make suggestions to the right people. The next Valentino right in their midst and they're wasting me. And Josefa won't help me. After all I've done for her. We could be so happy, all of us, if she would just help me.

(JOSEFA *enters from street.* MIGUEL *glares at her and exits into the house.* AMBER *and* JOSEFA *stare at each other.* AMBER *smiles at* JOSEFA, *and nods in the direction of the cigarette stash.*)

AMBER: Go ahead, have a smoke. What? You thought I didn't know?

(JOSEFA *hesitates, takes out her cigarettes and lights one.*)

AMBER: Gimme one, too.

(AMBER *and* JOSEFA *smoke together.*)

AMBER: You've lost that baby fat, you've gone and become pretty on me.

JOSEFA: No, I haven't.

AMBER: Yes, you have. You weren't supposed to do that.

(AMBER *and* JOSEFA *share a small laugh.*)

AMBER: I'm sure you must have noticed that men look at you differently now. *(She smooths* JOSEFA's *hair.)* Do you like it? *(*JOSEFA *is silent.)* It's okay to like it. …Your father needs your help, Josefa.

JOSEFA: I've already helped him, Mami.

AMBER: Sssh. Now, what's the point of being a pretty girl if you never use it. It's not gonna last forever, Josefa. It's over so quickly. It's the little bit of power you have. Use it. *(She exits into the house.)*

(Lights change from stars to dawn. JOSEFA *crosses to a backyard* CHRIS *enters from inside a house in his bathrobe and pajamas.)*

JOSEFA: Good morning.

CHRIS: *(Startled)* Jesus Christ! What are you doing out here?

JOSEFA: Good morning.

CHRIS: Good morning. How did you find out where I live?

JOSEFA: I looked it up. Montalvo Street. You know, if you Americans are going to keep our names for your streets you could at least—

CHRIS: What do you want?

JOSEFA: —learn how to pronounce them.

CHRIS: I'll get right on it. *(Silence)* Is there anything else?

JOSEFA: I'm cold.

*(*CHRIS *takes off his bathrobe and drapes it over her shoulders. He stares at her.)*

CHRIS: How old are you again?

JOSEFA: Jail bait.

*(*CHRIS *takes an involuntary step back.* JOSEFA *smiles.)*

CHRIS: Have my neighbors seen you out here?

(JOSEFA *shakes her head "no".)*

CHRIS: Maybe we should go inside.

(JOSEFA *nods, "yes".)*

CHRIS: Come here.

(JOSEFA *approaches him. They are about to kiss, she stops him.)*

JOSEFA: My father's option?

(CHRIS *nods, they kiss.* JOSEFA *heads for the door with him behind her.)*

CHRIS: Look, uh, I'm sorry about what I said before.

JOSEFA: It's better when you don't talk. *(She enters his house.)*

CHRIS: Right.

(CHRIS *follows* JOSEFA.)

(Song: Dearly Beloved *is heard from inside the* TORRES *house.* AMBER *sits on the porch steps, the music washing over her. She drinks from her flask. She gets up and dances a little by herself, she is a little tipsy and it shows. Lights come up in house to reveal* MIGUEL *dancing by himself. He holds out his hand and* JOSEFA *joins him. They continue their slow, romantic dance.* CHRIS *approaches porch. He is dressed for an evening on the town and carries a dress box.* AMBER *quickly hides her flask.)*

CHRIS: Good evening.

AMBER: Christopher, don't you look nice.

CHRIS: Don't mind me, finish your drink. Even the maid should have a night off.

AMBER: *(Sharply)* I'm not the maid.

CHRIS: Just a joke. A bad one. Where's Josefa?

AMBER: They're still rehearsing. They have a bit in a Kay Francis picture. Miguel says this is the one that's going to make everybody sit up and take notice.

CHRIS: Ah.

AMBER: I'm not allowed to watch them rehearse. Isn't that funny? Miguel says I make them nervous. *(Indicating dress box)* Is that a new dress?

CHRIS: Gotta show our girl off.

AMBER: Of course.

CHRIS: Could you maybe hurry her along? We've got a party to go to.

AMBER: No one hurries her along when she's dancing with her father. They're in their own little world. *(From inside the house)*

MIGUEL: The arch still isn't right.

JOSEFA: I'm going back as far as I can.

MIGUEL: Go back less, melt more. Come on.

(MIGUEL holds JOSEFA, she arches her back.)

MIGUEL: Less, less. Come on. Melt into my arms.

(JOSEFA does.)

MIGUEL: See, you're barely in my arms now.

(JOSEFA is not looking at MIGUEL.)

MIGUEL: Now, look at me. Remember, all good dancing is done with the eyes.

(JOSEFA looks at MIGUEL.)

MIGUEL: Just like this. We hold this pose.

(JOSEFA reaches up, gently touches MIGUEL's face.)

MIGUEL: ...Good. ...Good girl. Okay, now up. *(He helps her stand.)* You come from a long line of dancers, Josefa.

I'll be the first one to make it big, but there's no reason you can't have a little bit of success, too.

(MIGUEL *turns off the music.*)

JOSEFA: If you have it, then that's enough, Papi.

MIGUEL: *(More to himself than to her)* When did you get to be so good?

JOSEFA: What?

MIGUEL: I can talk to you now. One dancer to another.

JOSEFA: Thank you, papi.

MIGUEL: It's funny, when I dance with you I get to wear a suit, when I dance by myself they stick me all the way in the back. Are you tired?

JOSEFA: No.

MIGUEL: Let's do it again.

(Back on the front porch)

AMBER: You want me to put the dress in her room?

CHRIS: If you wouldn't mind.

AMBER: I'm sure it's a very, very pretty dress. For a pretty girl. Such a pretty girl.

(AMBER takes the dress box and walks to the house. She fumbles a bit.)

CHRIS: You okay?

AMBER: Of course I am. I'm a dancer, Christopher, not like her. I'm a real dancer. You know, she use to wear my hand me downs. My old dresses were good enough for her, but no more. Not any more. *(She takes the dress box and hits it against the wall, the dress spills out.)* She is living my life! Mine! And I gave it to her. I gave her my life.

(CHRIS goes to AMBER.)

AMBER: I'm sorry. I'm so sorry. I'm sure it's not ripped or anything.

(JOSEFA *and* MIGUEL *enter the porch.*)

JOSEFA: Mami, what happened? Are you okay?

AMBER: Yeah, of course. I tripped a little, that's all. Look at the pretty dress Christopher brought you. Say thank you.

JOSEFA: Thank you.

AMBER: That's a nice young lady. I raised her right. Let's go try it on. On you. Let's try it on you.

(JOSEFA *helps her stand.*)

JOSEFA: Careful, Mami, come on.

(*They exit.* MIGUEL *and* CHRIS *are left alone.* CHRIS *lets out a long whistle.*)

MIGUEL: What's that supposed to mean?

CHRIS: Nothing.

MIGUEL: My wife has a medical condition.

(CHRIS *nods.*)

CHRIS: Uh huh.

MIGUEL: You planning another late night?

CHRIS: This is an important party.

MIGUEL: They're all important parties.

CHRIS: It's important Josefa get seen.

MIGUEL: You didn't even ask me if she could go.

CHRIS: Sorry.

MIGUEL: She's not her own boss. She lives in my house, she follows my rules.

CHRIS: You know, somehow I don't think this would be a problem if I had managed to get an invitation for you, too.

(Silence)

MIGUEL: *(Calling into the house)* Don't bother with that dress, Josefa. You're not going anywhere tonight.

(JOSEFA comes to the screen door holding the dress up in front of her. MIGUEL enters, yanks it from her and throws it on the floor as he exits. He goes inside, slamming the screen door shut behind him. CHRIS exits. JOSEFA picks up the dress, holds it in front of her and slowly begins dancing by herself. Her hands touch her breasts. Her dance steps become slower and smaller. MIGUEL enters, he doesn't see her in the semi shadows. She watches him dance by himself. He holds out his hand in her direction, she is about to take it when AMBER bursts through the door, she and MIGUEL dance as JOSEFA watches them. MIGUEL keeps looking at JOSEFA, it is clear she is the one he wants to dance with, not AMBER. At the end of the dance AMBER tries to strike a romantic pose with MIGUEL, who turns his head. JOSEFA disappears into the house.)

(Lights out on MIGUEL and AMBER, up on CHRIS and STUART.)

STUART: Hey congratulations! Kramer wants to set up a meeting with you and the girl.

CHRIS: What?

STUART: Josefa. She's yours, right?

CHRIS: Of course she's mine.

(JOSEFA enters.)

STUART: Kramer kinda likes her. All these years of bringing in losers and you finally get a keeper. Oh, and don't forget you'll have to bring her father.

CHRIS: Why? What for?

STUART: She's still a minor, isn't she? He'll have to sign everything. He's not gonna be a problem, is he?

CHRIS: No, of course not.

STUART: You're one lucky dog, you bastard. *(He exits.)*

*(*CHRIS *takes a ring off his finger, looks at* JOSEFA.*)*

CHRIS: What do you say?

JOSEFA: Sure.

(Music: Someone's Rocking My Dreamboat *by Orrin Tucker. Lights fade on them come up on the* TORRES *front porch, where* MIGUEL *sits, polishing his shoes and* AMBER *is fanning herself.* JOSEFA *and* CHRIS *walk to the porch from the street.)*

CHRIS: We're married.

*(*MIGUEL *stands, faces* CHRIS, AMBER *hugs* JOSEFA.*)*

AMBER: My baby! My baby's married! This is wonderful!

JOSEFA: Did I make you happy, Mami?

AMBER: My baby, of course, but you should have told us. We're gonna give a big party, Miguel, congratulate our baby, big party for you, she's married. You should have told us. You could have told me, at least.

JOSEFA: I'm sorry. It happened so fast, didn't it Chris?

MIGUEL: When did it happen?

JOSEFA: Today.

MIGUEL: Where?

AMBER: Miguel, come on, come on let's get some

*(*MIGUEL *slams his shoe against the door.)*

MIGUEL: I said where?!

AMBER: champagne.

*(*CHRIS *puts his arm around* JOSEFA.*)*

CHRIS: Nevada. She's of age there, you know. A friend of mine flew us out there. I pulled some strings and got us married an hour after we touched ground. I was afraid this little angel would change her mind. She was the prettiest little bride. My angel.

MIGUEL: Just remember, she was my angel first.

AMBER: Our angel, honey. I have some champagne in the house.

CHRIS: Oh good, some of your wonderful champagne. Please, allow me. Give you folks a little chance to talk.

(CHRIS *turns to leave.*)

AMBER: Hey, kiss your bride. You two haven't been married long enough to forget to kiss each other.

(CHRIS *hurriedly kisses* JOSEFA *and enters the house.*)

AMBER: Look how embarrassed he is in front of his in-laws.

(MIGUEL *walks to the other end of the porch.*)

AMBER: You love him, right?

JOSEFA: Who?

AMBER: Your husband. I had no idea you were so in love with him. You never talked about him that way. Then again you were always such a quiet girl. What a good little secret keeper my Josefa is. Didn't even tell me she was in love.

(JOSEFA *nods.* AMBER *takes out her flask and toasts* JOSEFA.)

AMBER: Ssshh. We'll have our own little toast. To you. To you and Christopher. *(She drinks and passes the flask to* JOSEFA.*)* Just one sip, but don't get spoiled. You've made me so happy.

JOSEFA: Did I, Mami?

AMBER: A toast to your wedding night. Oh, it's all right, don't be embarrassed. He'll know what to do. Men always know what to do.

JOSEFA: And I wouldn't, right, Mami?

(AMBER *turns to stare at* MIGUEL, *he turns to exit.* JOSEFA *takes another drink.*)

AMBER: Hey one! One sip!

JOSEFA: Where are you going, papi?

MIGUEL: A walk. I just need to walk.

JOSEFA: You're not gonna congratulate me, papi?

MIGUEL: Congratulations.

JOSEFA: You're not gonna kiss me?

AMBER: Ah. Isn't that sweet. I hope you have a marriage just like ours.

(CHRIS *taps the door with his foot,* AMBER *hurries to help him.*)

JOSEFA: *(Softly, to* MIGUEL.*)* Do you love Mami?

MIGUEL: Of course. Do you love Chris?

(AMBER *helps* CHRIS *give out the glasses.* AMBER *kisses* JOSEFA. CHRIS *and* MIGUEL *awkwardly shake hands.* AMBER *throws her arms around* CHRIS's *neck.* MIGUEL *and* JOSEFA *stare at each other.*)

AMBER: A toast to the happy couple. Come on, Miguel, make a toast, say something. Look how cute, he's speechless. His only daughter is a married woman now. She's leaving home. Forever.

(MIGUEL *downs his drink.*)

AMBER: And ever.

(MIGUEL *takes* AMBER's *drink and downs it,* CHRIS *holds his away.*)

AMBER: His little girl.

(JOSEFA *takes a short sip, gives the rest of the drink to her father, who downs it.*)

(KRAMER's *office.*)

KRAMER: Let's not get too excited here but I see a real possible potential for promise.

CHRIS: You know she's a real hard worker. Beautiful, too.

KRAMER: She's pretty. Stop selling. Just married, dear?

JOSEFA: Yes, sir.

(KRAMER *smiles at* CHRIS.)

KRAMER: I'm sure it'll be a wise first marriage for both of you. I've got a little wedding present for you, dear. A brand new contract. We're tearing up your old one. We're going to groom you. Build you up. Make you a somebody. Aren't you the lucky girl?

CHRIS: She sure is.

STUART: Yes she is.

JOSEFA: Yes, sir.

KRAMER: A little cheap, but we'll take care of that. Now, let's start with your name. Josefa's an ugly name.

STUART: Hideous.

CHRIS: We could shorten it to Josie.

JOSEFA: No, I [don't like that.]

KRAMER: (*Cutting her off*) No, my first wife was a Josie. She was a bitch.

CHRIS: Okay, forget Josie.

JOSEFA: I have a name.

KRAMER: For a maid you have a name.

CHRIS: We're moving to the next level, Josefa. How about Jo?

KRAMER: No, too masculine I want a name that will make men want to fuck her.

JOSEFA: I have

CHRIS: Her mother's name is Amber.

JOSEFA: a name.

KRAMER: How's that again?

JOSEFA: I have a

CHRIS: Her mother's name.

KRAMER: *(To* JOSEFA*)* Not you, him.

CHRIS: Amber.

KRAMER: Amber.

STUART: Sexy name.

KRAMER: Fills up your mouth. Amber.

JOSEFA: No.

KRAMER: Amber Towers.

STUART: I like it.

JOSEFA: I don't want that name.

CHRIS: You'll get used to it, honey.

JOSEFA: No, I don't want it.

CHRIS: It's a very pretty [name.]

STUART: *(Cutting him off)* Sexy. A sexy name.

JOSEFA: I don't want her name!! *(Silence)* Please.

KRAMER: *(To* CHRIS*)* Tell her if she says one more word you're both fired. Do you understand me?

*(*CHRIS *nods.)*

KRAMER: Her name is Amber Towers.

JOSEFA: no.

*(*CHRIS *reaches for* JOSEFA *who pushes his hand away.)*

CHRIS: Jo—uh Amber, please, just shut up, please, okay?

KRAMER: Listen to your pimp husband, dear.

JOSEFA: There is no one is this room named Amber.

CHRIS: She'll be Amber. Trust me.

KRAMER: Not here she won't. Good luck.

(KRAMER *exits,* STUART *is about to follow him.* CHRIS *grabs his arm.*)

CHRIS: Talk to him. Please.

(CHRIS *follows* STUART *out.* JOSEFA *is left alone.*)

(*Lights up on* CHRIS *showing up at the* TORRES *home. He carries two suitcases. Sets them down as* MIGUEL, *in a tuxedo, enters porch from the house.* JOSEFA *enters, stands by the porch.*)

CHRIS: I don't know what you've heard but this is only temporary.

We'll be out of here before you know it. I've got everything under control, this is just a little setback that's all.

(MIGUEL *motions to the door with his head,* CHRIS *picks up his suitcase and goes into the house.* JOSEFA *stands by her suitcase. Silence*)

MIGUEL: When did they fire you?

JOSEFA: Three months ago.

MIGUEL: It was four.

JOSEFA: If you know, why did you ask? (*Silence*)
Where's Mami?

MIGUEL: She's asleep.

JOSEFA: Is she drunk?

MIGUEL: I said she's asleep.

JOSEFA: I just don't want her to get sick all over herself, that's all.

MIGUEL: She'll be fine.

(Silence)

JOSEFA: Chris is going to set me up at another studio. He says any day now he'll get me a contract. We'll be out of your way soon. *(She picks up her suitcase.)*

MIGUEL: He told me you were fired because you wouldn't take your mother's name.

(Silence)

JOSEFA: What are you working on?

MIGUEL: Nothing. A Constance Bennett picture. I get to ask her to dance. She turns me down.

JOSEFA: *Niña estupida.*

MIGUEL: She can't dance anyway.

(Music: The Andrew Sisters singing Apple Blossom Time starts from inside the house.)

MIGUEL: Your mother's up.

(MIGUEL begins to dance. JOSEFA picks up her bag, heads to the porch.)

MIGUEL: Why wouldn't you take her name?

JOSEFA: Why do you think?

(MIGUEL stops dancing. Slowly he begins again.)

MIGUEL: I don't. I just dance.

(JOSEFA looks down. She joins MIGUEL. They dance side by side, not looking at each other. They are two people trying desperately not to dance together, but they have to. They face each other, moving perfectly together. As the music nears the end, MIGUEL picks up JOSEFA, she rests her head on his chest, and he carries her into the house as the song ends.)

(Blackout)

END OF ACT ONE

ACT TWO

(As lights come up, there is a tight spotlight on MIGUEL *and* JOSEFA, *who begin to dance, almost frenetically to the swing music that plays. Their new "act" will be much more All American. The spotlight widens and now includes* AMBER *who watches from behind the screen door, ironing. The only available space for* MIGUEL *and* JOSEFA *to dance is on the porch.* CHRIS *is inside the house, yelling into the phone, fighting to be heard over the music. He and* AMBER *are practically on top of each other as he paces and she irons and hangs up shirts.)*

CHRIS: *(Into phone)* No, listen to me, she's gorgeous... *(Throwing an angry look at* MIGUEL*)* Gorgeous! No, really...this girl is money in the bank... *(Loudly, to* AMBER*)* Could we turn the music down a bit!

*(*AMBER *ignores him, staring at* MIGUEL *and* JOSEFA *who continue dancing.* JOSEFA *makes a mistake and* AMBER *immediately steps in to show her how it's done. She is not trying to help, more like reclaim her rightful place. Once* MIGUEL *sees that* JOSEFA *has gotten the step he motions for her to come back to the dance, and he releases* AMBER *who catches her breath as she glares at him, and goes back to her ironing.)*

CHRIS: *(Into phone)* You're gonna thank me... Come on, this is me...

(The rest of the sentence is lost under the music. He screams into the phone.)

CHRIS: I said, this is me! You're old pal! No, no, you heard wrong! Kramer's nuts about her!

(MIGUEL *and* JOSEFA *continue dancing.* AMBER *throws* MIGUEL's *shirt on the ground and stops* JOSEFA, *insisting she's made a mistake. She cuts in and starts dancing with* MIGUEL, *who after a few step goes back to* JOSEFA.)

CHRIS: *(Covering the phone mouth piece and yelling out)* Hey! I'm trying to work here!

(CHRIS *is ignored.* AMBER *again tries to cut in, but* MIGUEL *turns* JOSEFA *so that* AMBER *can't.* AMBER *jumps in anyway and suddenly* MIGUEL *is dancing with both women.* AMBER *does a step that locks out* JOSEFA, *but* MIGUEL *turns and continues his dance with* JOSEFA. AMBER *fumbles then storms inside and turns off the music.)*

MIGUEL: Hey!

CHRIS: *(Loudly)* Yeah, well— *(Realizing the music is gone, lowers his voice)* —thanks for nothing.

MIGUEL: Put that music back on, we're in the middle of rehearsing! Amber!

(CHRIS *hangs up.* MIGUEL *heads to the door just as* CHRIS *heads to the porch. They practically bump into each other.)*

CHRIS: *(Trying to hold his temper)* Miguel, I realize I'm only a guest here, but I'm trying to work—

MIGUEL: *(Cutting him off, he extends his hand to* JOSEFA*)* Come on. We'll do it without the music.

CHRIS: Hey! I'm working! I'm out there everyday trying to sell Josefa! Calling people, trying to set up appointments, I could use a little help—

MIGUEL: *(Cutting him off)* What people?! You don't know anybody! Who do you know? Who do you know, Mister Big Shot?

CHRIS: So what's your plan? Stick her in some dive with you in Tiajuana dancing for drunks and making fifty bucks a show?

MIGUEL: Then bring some money into this house! I'm the only one making any money here. You like to eat? She's gotta dance.

CHRIS: How about all the money she made when she was under contract, huh? She never saw a dime of that. That money belonged to her and it belongs to me. Give me everything my wife made when she was under contract—

MIGUEL: She wasn't your wife then!

CHRIS: And we'll both be outta here!

MIGUEL: You can go whenever you want. Josefa's staying. We're gonna do the act again and if you don't like it [that's too bad.]

CHRIS: *(Cutting him off)* No, Miguel. I'm her husband. I'm the one who tells her what to do now. Not you.

(AMBER enters with her castanets, stands in the doorway. MIGUEL close to punching CHRIS out, goes into the house. CHRIS follows, stands in the doorway and yells for MIGUEL and JOSEFA's benefit.)

CHRIS: And for the record, I remember your act. I was there, remember? How old was your daughter? How old was daddy's little girl?! *(He goes past AMBER and enters house.)*

JOSEFA: I'm sorry.

AMBER: For what? Don't be silly. They're just two roosters in a hen house. *(She clicks her castanets.)* One rooster two many. Men don't like to share. Anything. *(She clicks her castanets.)* This house never seemed so small to me before. Your room so close to ours. Can you hear us at night? We can hear you. As if we were right there with you.

(AMBER *clicks her castanets as she circles* JOSEFA. MIGUEL *enters.* AMBER *turns and sees* MIGUEL.)

AMBER: Miguel, look what I found. (*She clicks them, looks from* MIGUEL *to* JOSEFA.) Remember Miguel? Your father gave them to me. He carved them himself. Even put my initials on them. See? So that everyone would know that they were mine. They belong to me. (*She clicks them.*) I'm good, huh Miguel? Aren't I still good?

CHRIS: Josefa. Hey, Josefa. We're on our way! I got us a job.

(JOSEFA *doesn't move.*)

CHRIS: Well don't just stand there. Come on.

AMBER: Don't keep your husband waiting, dear.

(JOSEFA *exits.*)

CHRIS: (*To* MIGUEL) Didn't I tell you something would turn up? Looks like you'll be doing a single act in Tiajuana, Miguel.

(CHRIS *exits into house. Silence*)

AMBER: Chris got her a job. That's what you wanted him to do, right? I mean, it's good news, right? ...I was thinking, if you still wanted to do the act, maybe you and I should do it. What do you think? Am I crazy?

MIGUEL: Amber, we haven't danced together in years.

AMBER: But it could help us, help the family. Just let me help, Miguel. That's all I want.

(MIGUEL *takes her hand, kisses it.*)

AMBER: I know to favor your left shoulder because your right one starts to hurt after an hour, I know to slow my turns so that you'll be there to catch me, how to spin without ever taking my eyes off your face. I remember. I remember everything, Miguel.

MIGUEL: That was a lifetime ago. I'm so much older now.

AMBER: Ssssh. No. Never.

MIGUEL: I was so much younger when I was dancing with Josefa.

AMBER: *(Gently touches his head.)* Yes. Yes you were.

(Music up. Lights out on them, up on Studio as JOSEFA, *in a showgirl outfit, finishes her dance.)*

VOICE: Cut. All right let's set up for the girl's close up.

*(*CHRIS *enters, drapes a fur coat over* JOSEFA*'s shoulders.)*

JOSEFA: What's this?

CHRIS: Sssh. Never mind. Just want to make sure they know you're a star.

JOSEFA: I'm a chorus girl.

CHRIS: You got a line. Let's hear it.

JOSEFA: Hi, my name is Ruby. You can ask—

CHRIS: You didn't wink.

JOSEFA: Sorry.

CHRIS: Josefa, it's all about the wink. You gotta wink. That's what sells it. It's all about making you stand out.

JOSEFA: Hi, my name is Ruby. *(She winks.)* You can ask me out—

CHRIS: And pop your gum.

JOSEFA: I don't have any—

CHRIS: *(Handing her gum, which she begins to chew.)* Here. Look, you're one of six chorus girls, but you're the one who got the line at the end of the number and we want to draw attention to you. You're the star of the number. You've got to think of yourself that way so they will.

JOSEFA: I'm a extra.

CHRIS: Don't say that! Don't ever say that. You are not an extra. You know why? Because I'm not married to an extra.

JOSEFA: Okay, okay.

CHRIS: I had to pull in every favor I had left to get you this.

JOSEFA: Chris…I'm afraid.

CHRIS: You'll be fine.

JOSEFA: I never had to say anything before, all I had to do was dance.

CHRIS: Just do it like I taught you.

JOSEFA: I don't want to say the line, please, I did the dance, that's enough.

CHRIS: Are you crazy?!

VOICE: Josie Malloy.

CHRIS: We're right here. *(To* JOSEFA*)* Look, you're not just gonna be some dancer in the background or the local peasant every time they set a picture south of the border. I am not going to spend the rest of my life living with your parents.

JOSEFA: Then get a job.

CHRIS: You are my job. *(He takes her fur coat.)* Miss Malloy is ready.

VOICE: We're just gonna pick it up from the end of the dance.

*(*CHRIS *rushes off camera range.)*

VOICE: Okay, play back music.

(Music starts. JOSEFA *begins dancing.)*

VOICE: Not yet.

(JOSEFA *continues dancing.*)

CHRIS: *(Hisses)* Josefa. ...Uh, Josie...

VOICE: Fine. Just let her go. Quiet please. *Dancing Chorines of 1938,* scene eight, take one, action.

(CHRIS *nods to* JOSEFA. *As the music ends, she stops, looks straight into the camera and begins to vamp wildly.*)

JOSEFA: Hi, my name is Ruby. You can ask me out tonight—

VOICE: Cut. Go back to the beginning. Don't move around so much, slow it down a bit.

(JOSEFA *looks to* CHRIS *for guidance.*)

VOICE: Take it again.

JOSEFA: *(Thrown)* —tomorrow and twice—

VOICE: From the beginning.

CHRIS: *(Hisses)* The wink.

VOICE: Keep going.

JOSEFA: *(Looking down)* Hi, my name is—

VOICE: Look up.

JOSEFA: Hi, my name is Ruby. *(She does a huge wink.)*

VOICE: Lose the wink. Go back.

JOSEFA: What? Uh, hi my name is Ruby—

VOICE: Open your eyes.

JOSEFA: Hi, my name is Ruby—

VOICE: But don't look in the camera. Jesus, she can dance, but she just can't talk.

CHRIS: No, she can talk, trust me, really, she talks all the time.

VOICE: From her last few steps. Playback music. Action.

JOSEFA: *(Barely audible in the beginning, rising in volume at the end as she really struggles to do it.)* Hi, my name is Ruby. You can ask me out tonight—

(CHRIS frantically chews gum, JOSEFA follows his lead.)

JOSEFA: —tomorrow and twice on Sunday— *(Her hand suddenly flies up to her mouth.)*

CHRIS: *(Hisses)* You swallowed the gum?!

(A panic stricken JOSEFA nods.)

VOICE: Okay, get the other girl in here. This is taking too long.

CHRIS: No, this is her bit! She's the lead in this.

VOICE: Get him off my set.

(JOSEFA is about to leave.)

VOICE: Hold on. Let's move in tight on her face.

(The spotlight narrows on JOSEFA's face.)

VOICE: She's got a pretty face. Just do exactly what I tell you, little girl. Tilt your head down a little, that will stop the shaking.

(JOSEFA does.)

VOICE: Too much.

(JOSEFA lifts her head a little.)

VOICE: See? Nice and steady. Okay, now raise your eyes and say your line.

JOSEFA: What?

VOICE: Say the line.

JOSEFA: Hi, my name is Ruby. You can ask me out tonight, tomorrow and twice on Sunday.

VOICE: Gimme a small smile.

JOSEFA: *(She does.)* Cause I don't work on Monday.

VOICE: Thank you. Cut. That's it. Set up for the next one.

JOSEFA: That's it?

VOICE: That's it.

(CHRIS puts the fur coat on her shoulders, smiles broadly for everyone as he whispers in JOSEFA's ear.)

CHRIS: Come on. I gotta get that fur back by three.

(The spotlight remains. JOSEFA hurries back into the light for a second, takes a bow, and then exits. As her bow slowly begins to fade in the spotlight, an estatic CHRIS is having a celebratory drink on the porch recounting the day to AMBER.)

CHRIS: They loved her! I thought they were gonna sign her right on the spot. I mean, they didn't say it, but I could tell.

AMBER: That's wonderful, Christopher.

CHRIS: *(Over her)* And a big, beautiful close up. Did I tell you that already? Just her face. We hadn't even planned on that. The director took time with her because he knows she's got something. Once her movie comes out we'll be able to pick and choose from offers. Studios are going to be lining up for us. This little piece of film changes everything.

(MIGUEL arrives from Empire Studios.)

MIGUEL: Celebrating already?

AMBER: Miguel, let Christopher tell you all about Josefa's day. Everything went perfectly.

MIGUEL: Did it?

AMBER: And to celebrate, the four of us are going out tonight. We're going dancing.

MIGUEL: Go inside for a little bit. Chris and I need to talk.

AMBER: Okay, you men talk, but don't say no Miguel. Please. I don't want to hear no tonight. *(She kisses MIGUEL and begins singing to herself as she hurries into the house.)*

CHRIS: Takes so little to make her happy, doesn't it?

MIGUEL: I know all about Josefa's day.

CHRIS: How about that? Her film is still wet and people are already talking about her.

MIGUEL: They certainly are.

CHRIS: This is just killing you, isn't it? Well, that's just a bonus.

MIGUEL: Mister Kramer found out you changed her name and got her a job.

CHRIS: Good news travels fast.

MIGUEL: He's not gonna let her work anywhere again.

CHRIS: *(Sucker punched)* What?

MIGUEL: Call around. See if any studio will touch her. Or you.

(CHRIS sits heavily on the porch step.)

MIGUEL: Oh, and by the way, he got them to cut her line from the movie. *(Silence)* Isn't it amazing what a small town Hollywood is?

CHRIS: It wasn't even at his studio.

MIGUEL: I guess he just has more friends than you do. *(He sits next to CHRIS, takes his drink, finishes it.)*

MIGUEL: Now, if I were you, this is what I would do. I would just pack up and leave. Maybe try New York.

(CHRIS looks at MIGUEL.)

MIGUEL: Trust me, you won't be missed.

(Silence)

CHRIS: If you were me, if you were me...you'd find another way in. You'd just introduce your daughter to somebody else. That's how you got what you wanted. All it took was the promise of a screen test. Something the Mrs doesn't know about, I'm sure.

(MIGUEL *stares at* CHRIS *as* CHRIS *stands.*)

CHRIS: I still have something people want. My wife. Thanks, Miguel. Josefa will know what to do. She'll put up a fight, but you know she'll do as she's told. You taught her well.

(CHRIS *steps off porch, lights shift as he walks to* PRODUCER.)

CHRIS: *(To* PRODUCER*)* You've met my wife, haven't you?

(CHRIS *extends his arm as* MIGUEL *did when* JOSEFA *would join him in dance.* JOSEFA *enters, shakes the producer's hand, then looks down to the floor, a dance begins in which it is made clear that* JOSEFA *is traded from man to man. When her dance ends, lights slowly go out on her and up to dim on the porch where* MIGUEL *sits smoking. Enter* AMBER *who begins dancing by herself, snapping her castanets. Her longing and frustration are mixed with desire.* AMBER *dances around* MIGUEL, *but is ignored. She reenters house in defeat.* JOSEFA *enters scene.* MIGUEL *rises. Silence)*

MIGUEL: No luck?

JOSEFA: No, Papi. No luck.

MIGUEL: Did you walk back?

JOSEFA: Chris had other appointments.

(JOSEFA *sits on the step.* MIGUEL *sits at her feet, takes off her shoes and begins to massage her feet. She pulls back.*)

JOSEFA: What are you doing?

MIGUEL: You're a dancer. You should respect your feet more.

(JOSEFA *allows* MIGUEL's *massage to continue.*)

JOSEFA: No, Papi, you're the dancer.

MIGUEL: Did you and Chris have another fight?

(JOSEFA *looks away.*)

MIGUEL: You're not crying, are you?

JOSEFA: No.

MIGUEL: Because we both know you don't love him.

JOSEFA: Somebody in this damn house should be in love.

MIGUEL: I love your mother, I love you. *(Silence)* You love your mother, you love me. *(Silence)* I said you [love your mother.]

JOSEFA: I'm not deaf.

(Silence)

MIGUEL: What does Chris make you do?

JOSEFA: Nothing.

MIGUEL: Nothing?

JOSEFA: What did you make me do?

MIGUEL: Nothing.

JOSEFA: Same thing. *(She rises, is about to enter the house when she turns to* MIGUEL *in a rage and throws her shoes at him.)* What am I supposed to do!? Tell me. What am I supposed to do?

(AMBER *comes to the door when she hears the outburst.*)

JOSEFA: Please. Tell me. Please.

(MIGUEL *grabs* JOSEFA *and kisses her. Both of them momentarily lost in each other. They embrace.*)

MIGUEL: Let's go away.

JOSEFA: Where, Papi?

MIGUEL: To where we used to dance. To where you were still a girl. My girl. We would dance all night and everyone thought you were my wife. We'll go and never come back, we'll disappear. That's when I was happiest. We were both never happier than at that time.

(MIGUEL *holds* JOSEFA's *face in his hands.* CHRIS *arrives.* JOSEFA *and* MIGUEL *separate, but* MIGUEL *holds* CHRIS' *stare for a moment.* MIGUEL *turns, is about to enter the house when he sees* AMBER.)

AMBER: The studio called. They can use you. Night club scene. You'll need your tuxedo. I've laid it out on the bed.

MIGUEL: You see that, Chris? They're always going to call me, because I can do something. I have talent, unlike you. The day Josefa leaves you, what will you have? Nothing.

(CHRIS *eyes* JOSEFA.)

CHRIS: Who said anything about Josefa leaving?

MIGUEL: *(To* AMBER) Where are my onyx cuff links?

AMBER: In the night stand, where they always are.

(MIGUEL *enters house.* AMBER *stays on the porch.* CHRIS *goes to* JOSEFA's *cigarette stash, finds an empty box and angrily tosses it away.*)

JOSEFA: I'm all out.

CHRIS: I'm not blind. I can see that. *(Silence)* They repossessed the car.

JOSEFA: I'm sorry.

CHRIS: Finally cornered Kramer's guy outside the studio. Giving him the best hard sell of my life, laughing at his lame jokes, getting him on my side and my car's repossessed, right in front of him. In front of an assistant, for Christ's sake. *(Turning on* AMBER) Do you think we could have some privacy?! Would it be too much to ask if for one goddamn minute *(we could be alone?)*

(AMBER *hurries into the house before* CHRIS *can finish. Silence)*

JOSEFA: This is her house. Not yours.

CHRIS: It's not yours anymore, either. ...So, are you still mad? ...You looked real pretty today. Sometimes you're so beautiful I can't even look at you.

JOSEFA: Are you drunk?

CHRIS: Can't afford it. Cannot afford a fucking beer! How about that? ...You were supposed to be my ticket out.

JOSEFA: Maybe I'm just sleeping with the wrong men.

CHRIS: Well, you sorta have a history of that, don't you.

(JOSEFA *heads to the house.)*

CHRIS: Come here.

(JOSEFA *continues.* CHRIS *roughly grabs her wrists.)*

CHRIS: I said "Come here".

(JOSEFA *pushes* CHRIS *away. He grabs her and slams her against the wall.)*

CHRIS: Kramer's having a big party and we're crashing. I want you to smile, say thank you and please. You do anything, you make him know how sorry you are. Cause I will cut you, I will slice your face, you got that?

JOSEFA: You won't do that.

CHRIS: Maybe I'll get somebody to do it for me. I'm at the end of my rope, Josefa, I don't know what I'll do. You owe me. You hear me? Look at me! You owe me.

(JOSEFA *nods.* CHRIS *awkwardly holds her for a moment, then goes into the house.* JOSEFA *picks up her shoes, looks*

*at the house then runs off stage. LIghts shift to indicate
a darkened lobby of a movie theatre.* JOSEFA *arrives, still
carrying her shoes.)*

JOSEFA: One ticket, please.

*(*JOSEFA *enters movie theater, lights flicker across her face.
She sits and puts on her shoes. The music from the movie
swells up, she looks up. She rises from her seat and begins to
dance in front of the screen. She is transformed. As her dance
ends, she sits back in her seat and with one hand reaches
longingly towards the screen. Lights dim on her, come up
on porch.* CHRIS *paces in tuxedo pants, suspenders, and an
undershirt as* AMBER *finishes mending his dress shirt.)*

AMBER: There. Good as new.

CHRIS: Thanks.

AMBER: Always happy to help.

CHRIS: Yeah, I wish Josefa was a little more like you.

*(*AMBER *and* CHRIS *stare awkwardly at each other.)*

CHRIS: In some things.

*(*JOSEFA *arrives.* AMBER *looks away, enters house.* CHRIS *is
silent as* JOSEFA *watches him.)*

CHRIS: Get ready for Kramer's party. And put some
make up on, for Christ's sake. You look like you
haven't slept in a week.

JOSEFA: That's because I haven't.

CHRIS: We're not gonna argue about this, Josefa.

JOSEFA: You once said you couldn't take your eyes off
me when I was dancing.

CHRIS: I said a lot of things. I can't be expected to
remember all of them.

JOSEFA: I went to the movies. I saw myself dance. I
looked up at myself and I was made out of light and

movement and for the first time I thought, I'm good at this. I can dance.

CHRIS: The clock's ticking, Josefa.

JOSEFA: Dance with me. Please. You asked me to dance with you once, now I'm asking you. Please let me show you.

(CHRIS *grabs her roughly, does a few steps and releases her.*)

CHRIS: Happy? Now get ready.

(JOSEFA *doesn't move.*)

CHRIS: It doesn't matter that you can dance, Josefa. What matters is if they want you. Kramer has to want you. Look, everybody does it. You're not the only one.

JOSEFA: *(Cutting him off.)* No, not everybody—

CHRIS: *(Cutting her off)* What the hell makes you think you're special? *(Silence)* Seven thirty.

JOSEFA: ...I'll be ready. ...Did you ever love me?

CHRIS: *(Unable to look at her)* Josefa, I love you right now.

(CHRIS *continues getting ready.* JOSEFA *looks at him for a moment, then turns to the house.*)

JOSEFA: Mami, come help me pick my perfume.

(JOSEFA *exits into house. Music begins to play from inside the house. Lights slowly up on* AMBER, *as she goes to the vanity.* MIGUEL *steps out on the porch as* JOSEFA *appears at her mother's side and begins to get ready.* CHRIS *enters the porch from the house, in his tuxedo.*)

CHRIS: Car keys?

(MIGUEL *hesitates a second, takes them out of his pocket and tosses them to* CHRIS.)

MIGUEL: Nice tuxedo. Borrowed?

CHRIS: Stolen. *(He paces.)*

MIGUEL: You're a little jumpy tonight.

CHRIS: Not at all. Everything is under control.

MIGUEL: So what's your plan for tonight?

CHRIS: Crashing Kramer's party.

MIGUEL: Throwing her on the mercy of the big man?

CHRIS: Under it if need be.

(MIGUEL *slaps* CHRIS. *Silence)*

MIGUEL: Don't forget. I am her father. Go put some ice on that. You don't want that to swell up. Not tonight.

(CHRIS *storms into the house.* AMBER *and* JOSEFA *tense up at the sound of the slamming door.* CHRIS *enters.)*

AMBER: Isn't she beautiful, Christopher? How could any man resist her?

CHRIS: That's what we're banking on.

AMBER: You're a very lucky man.

CHRIS: Don't I know it.

CHRIS: Josefa, tonight, whatever it takes. I mean it. I'll wait in the car. Hurry.

JOSEFA: Mami, get my back.

(AMBER *zips up* JOSEFA.)

JOSEFA: Did you hear what Chris said?

AMBER: Isn't that music beautiful? Dance with me.

(JOSEFA *and* AMBER *begin to dance.)*

AMBER: You've been such a good daughter.

JOSEFA: Mami...when I went dancing with Papi across the border, when I became his partner

AMBER: Dancing partner.

JOSEFA: we would sometimes stay out overnight, spend the night [together].

AMBER: Because your father can't drive at night. He gets sleepy. Falls asleep the second his head hits the pillow.

JOSEFA: ...That's right, mami. The second.

AMBER: Always did. Always. ...My Miguel. You look pretty. No, tonight you look beautiful. Now when you enter the room, freeze in the doorway. Be shy and proud at the same time. A goddess should always make an entrance. *Mi Diosa.*

JOSEFA: I'm so tired, Mami.

AMBER: And when you dance remember your partner is the most important person in the world. Make him look good. Give the dance to him.

JOSEFA: What if it doesn't work, if it never works?

AMBER: Ssshh. This is the part where he loves you and all the sacrifice is worth it. All the times you had to disappear don't matter. He's tall and perfect thanks to you. You have to discover what the man needs you to be, then be it. Be it as if your life depended on it and it was the most natural thing in the world.

JOSEFA: We've never danced together before, mami.

AMBER: No. I guess I was afraid of you.

JOSEFA: Everything I learned about dance I learned from you. Your shoulders, your hands, they were my bible. You were the best one of us all, Mami. Don't you miss it?

AMBER: I miss being held.

(Car horn is heard.)

AMBER: If he had to choose between us, who do you think he'd pick? *(Silence)* Not a night goes by that I don't ask myself "who would he pick?"

JOSEFA: ...You, of course.

AMBER: No. With you, he was successful, even if it was just for a little bit. I couldn't give him that. You're the color of his dreams, Josefa, I'm the color of his truth.

JOSEFA: Mami—

AMBER: Sssh, it's just the maid, saying good night. You're ready now, Josefa. Please, don't come back.

(AMBER *and* JOSEFA *kiss.* AMBER *stands in doorway as* JOSEFA *leaves the house.* AMBER *exits into house as* MIGUEL *enters porch, he puts a flower behind* JOSEFA'*s ear.*)

MIGUEL: I'll wait up for you and after everyone's asleep, we'll leave. Tonight. It has to be tonight. It'll all be for the better, I promise you.

(JOSEFA *exits.* KRAMER'*s party.* JOSEFA *stands off to the side as* CHRIS *approaches* KRAMER.)

CHRIS: Hello, Mister Kramer.

KRAMER: Who'd you slip a fin to?

CHRIS: I can't tell you that, I'd get him in trouble.

KRAMER: Fired.

CHRIS: Fired. See? That's trouble right there. Nice party.

KRAMER: It was.

CHRIS: Josefa's here.

KRAMER: I don't know a Josefa.

CHRIS: Amber's here.

KRAMER: I don't know her either.

CHRIS: She's learned her lesson, Mister Kramer. Your banning her really worked.

(KRAMER *takes a champagne flute from a nearby table, he sees that* CHRIS *doesn't dare.*)

KRAMER: (*Indicating the champagne.*) Oh for Christ's sake, don't hover over it, go ahead and take one.

(CHRIS *does.*)

(*Lights shift to* JOSEFA *who is trying to disappear.* STUART *approaches her, with a glass of champagne and another one for her.*)

STUART: Champagne?

JOSEFA: No thanks.

STUART: Take one. They're free.

(JOSEFA *smiles, takes the champagne.* STUART *indicates* KRAMER *and* CHRIS.)

STUART: Not going too well over there.

JOSEFA: I knew it wouldn't work.

STUART: You could change Kramer's mind, you know.

JOSEFA: I'm the one he's angry at.

STUART: No. You're the one he wants.

(JOSEFA *looks at* STUART *for a moment, smiles.*)

JOSEFA: Tell me...

STUART: Stewie.

JOSEFA: Stuart. I bet you know everything about Mister Kramer.

(*Lights shift back to* KRAMER *and* CHRIS.)

CHRIS: Because of you no one, no one will hire her. Even the sub B studios on Poverty Row, they won't touch her. I mean, for programmers, for Christ's sake. Yeah, you certainly are a powerful man, Mister Kramer.

KRAMER: Let me tell you something,

CHRIS: Chris.

KRAMER: Did I ask? Let me tell you, do you think you or the little tramp you pimp from studio to studio are worth that much effort on my part? You don't exist to me. You dare give yourself me as an enemy? How the fuck do you think you rate that?

CHRIS: Then why won't anybody hire us?

KRAMER: Maybe she stinks in bed. You ever think of that?

(CHRIS grabs KRAMER's arm.)

KRAMER: What? All of a sudden you're a gentleman? Don't be stupid.

(CHRIS lets KRAMER go.)

KRAMER: Where is she?

CHRIS: Over there.

KRAMER: Pretty girl. Can dance a little. Dime a dozen. Enjoy the champagne. Get out of here before they start serving the hors d'oeuvres. They're expensive.

(lights shift to JOSEFA and STUART She takes the flower from behind her ear and gives it to him as CHRIS joins them. CHRIS shakes his head in defeat.)

CHRIS: Come on.

JOSEFA: Wait a second, now—

CHRIS: Josefa—

JOSEFA: Wait, let's see, I've slept with him and him and that one.

CHRIS: Stop it.

JOSEFA: The bald man over there, too. Yoo hoo.

CHRIS: Ssshh. For pete's sake, shut up.

JOSEFA: Who's Pete? Did I sleep with him, too? Though I never sleep with them. It's over in a few minutes.

CHRIS: Let's just get out of here.

JOSEFA: Does it bother you? Of course not. If it doesn't bother me, why should it bother you? And it doesn't bother me. It doesn't bother anybody.

CHRIS: That's enough.

(JOSEFA *sips her drink as she approaches* KRAMER. CHRIS *follows her, trying to stop her.*)

CHRIS: Josefa!

KRAMER: What an unexpected pleasure, Miss Whatever Your Name Is.

JOSEFA: Dance with me.

KRAMER: So sorry. I don't dance.

(JOSEFA *gives her glass to* CHRIS, *she takes* KRAMER'S *glass, takes a sip and also hands it to* CHRIS. KRAMER *turns to leave,* JOSEFA *positions herself by his side and arches as if he were holding her, the same way she did with* MIGUEL. *Song: Thinking Of You.*)

KRAMER: I don't like to look like a fool, miss.

JOSEFA: Keep your hand in the small of my back.

KRAMER: *(Hisses)* All right, that's enough.

JOSEFA: *(Whispers)* Everybody's watching us, Mister Kramer. *(She turns and folds perfectly into him.)* You can dance. Just watch how you dance with me.

(JOSEFA *leads* KRAMER *out to the dance floor and begins to dance, giving the dance to him as she did with* MIGUEL, *as her mother taught her. She makes* KRAMER *look graceful. For* JOSEFA, *no other man in the room exists except* KRAMER. *He begins to relax.*)

JOSEFA: Of course you can dance. You're perfect. Left. You're doing fine. Just keep looking into my eyes.

KRAMER: How old are you again?

JOSEFA: How old do you want me to be?

KRAMER: Good answer. Now here's a more difficult one. What's your name?

JOSEFA: Iris, it was your mother's name.

KRAMER: How did you know that?

JOSEFA: And you insisted it be my new name.

KRAMER: Did I?

JOSEFA: And I obeyed. You're so graceful, Mister Kramer. You're the most graceful man in the world.

KRAMER: How did you know it was my mother's name? *(He waves to someone as they dance.)* Been practicing, yeah. *(To* JOSEFA*)* My wife is in shock.

JOSEFA: You don't dance with her?

KRAMER: I don't do anything with her. You really are quite...beautiful.

JOSEFA: Sssh.

*(*JOSEFA *and* KRAMER's *dancing becomes more romantic. The song ends, she curtsies to him who acknowledges his guests' applause.)*

KRAMER: Thank you, thank you all. Please join us for dinner in the grand salon.

*(*JOSEFA *is about to leave.)*

KRAMER: Not so fast. You'll come to the studio tomorrow.

JOSEFA: Of course.

KRAMER: This...Chris.

JOSEFA: My husband.

KRAMER: You don't need him, do you?

JOSEFA: What time tomorrow?

KRAMER: Tell me, has everyone in town already had you?

JOSEFA: You're the only one I've danced with. You've had the best part of me.

CHRIS: Mr. Kramer, you two certainly looked good out there.

KRAMER: Of course you'll join us for dinner, Iris.

(KRAMER *offers his arm.* JOSEFA *looks at* CHRIS *one last time, before taking* KRAMER's *arm and exiting with him to her future.*)

(*Lights out on* JOSEFA *and* KRAMER. *Music: Rum And Coca Cola.* MIGUEL, *his skin darkened is dressed as a peasant. He does a bastardization of a Mexican hat dance. It should be painful to watch.*)

VOICE: Cut. Okay, good enough. Print. We're ready for you Miss Towers.

(MIGUEL *takes off his hat.* JOSEFA *appears at her most beautiful.* STUART *is giving* JOSEFA *her instructions when she realizes that the peasant is* MIGUEL.)

STUART: Okay, Iris, this shot is the set up for your solo dance. We'll do the lead in, you'll walk past the peasant, peasant does his bit, you enter night club looking for Judd. Then we'll pick up on your dance. Okay, let's go.

JOSEFA: (*To* MIGUEL) Papi...?

STUART: Iris dear.

MIGUEL: Don't keep the man waiting.

STUART: It's late in the day, dear. We just want to get this one last shot and your dance.

(JOSEFA *nods and walks off.*)

VOICE: *Happy Endings,* scene 42, take one. Rolling, action.

(JOSEFA *enters and walks past* MIGUEL.)

MIGUEL: So pretty.

(JOSEFA *stops and looks at her father.*)

STUART: No. Cut. Dear, smile and you keep going. You keep walking. Come on, let's get this one done and we can all go home.

(JOSEFA *goes to her mark.*)

STUART: And could the peasant be a little more peasanty? (*He dirties* MIGUEL's *costume.*) Also try to make it sound funnier, you know, kinda stupid. You know, "soo preetee", like that.

VOICE: Okay, let's go again. Rolling. Action.

(JOSEFA *enters.*)

MIGUEL: (*Not able to look up*) So pretty.

STUART: Oh come on, peasant, you have to look at her. Let's not stop. Iris, go back to your mark and reenter.

VOICE: Okay, action.

(JOSEFA *reenters.*)

MIGUEL: So preetee.

(JOSEFA *stops, unable to look at* MIGUEL, *can barely breathe.*)

STUART: Cut! Are you okay? Do you need a little break?

JOSEFA: I'm fine. I think I need to go home.

STUART: We just want to finish this bit, sweetheart.

JOSEFA: And we can finish it tomorrow. (*Ice*) Sweetheart.

(*Silence.* STUART *moves off.*)

MIGUEL: What are you doing? Finish the scene.

JOSEFA: They'll have to pay you for another day.

MIGUEL: (*Hisses*) Finish the goddamn scene!

JOSEFA: ...No.

VOICE: Peasant you're fine.

JOSEFA: He has—

MIGUEL: Shut up.

JOSEFA: —a name.

STUART: I'm sure he does, Miss Towers.

MIGUEL: *(To voice)* Peasant is fine. *(To* JOSEFA.*)* Do you think I want them to know my name? Do it as I taught you. *Mi niña. Mi niña estupida.*

VOICE: Can we do another take, Miss Towers?

MIGUEL: *(Whispers)* Please.

JOSEFA: ...Yes.

STUART: That's a girl.

VOICE: Okay, back on your mark. Holding for sound please.

*(*MIGUEL *and* JOSEFA *look straight out, waiting for their cue.)*

JOSEFA: How's Mami?

MIGUEL: The same.

JOSEFA: And you?

MIGUEL: Me? I'm a star.

JOSEFA: ...Do you miss me?

MIGUEL: To tell you the truth I never even think of you.

(Silence. They both know he is lying. MIGUEL *takes her hand, they hold hands briefly.* MIGUEL *watches as hair and make up people descend on* JOSEFA. *She is living out his dream. She returns to her mark.)*

VOICE: Quiet please. *Happy Endings,* scene 42, take 4. Camera rolling, action.

*(*JOSEFA *enters.* MIGUEL *looks up.)*

MIGUEL: So, so pretty.

(JOSEFA *turns to* MIGUEL *and smiles. He takes a small step towards her and then backs away.*)

(*Music up:* I Can Dream, Can't I?)

(JOSEFA *begins to dance, she is at her most beautiful. As she dances scrims appear around her, each with a different headline. Each headline should have enough time one from the other. The headlines should start after the* VOICE *for the coming attractions.*)

VOICE: Empire Pictures proudly presents your number one film favorite, Iris Towers in her most glorious picture ever! Join Iris as she discovers true love in her dazzling technicolor musical extravaganza *Happy Endings*! Yes Iris was never lovelier than in this fun filled romantic romp. She sings, she dances, she romances in this years sunniest hit, it's Iris Towers in Empire Pictures' *Happy Endings,* coming soon to a theater near you!

(*First Headline*: Film Favorite Iris Towers Hospitalized With Exhaustion)

(*Second Headline:* Iris Returns to Studio After 3rd Marriage Fails)

(*Third Headline:* Custody Battle for Towers, Children Placed in Foster Care)

(*Fourth Headline:* Actress, Drunk, Hysterical Escorted Off Plane)

(*Fifth Headline:* Alzheimer's Claims Screen Legend Iris Towers, Dead at 68)

(*Sixth Headline:* Fallece Iris Towers, *diosa eterna del cine.*)

(*Mist envelops the radiant* JOSEFA. *As the music ends,* JOSEFA *faces straight out, a small Mona Lisa like smile on her face. The spot light becomes smaller, almost like a close up of her face. As the lights slowly fade on her the last sound we hear is the sound of a film strip slapping against itself when it has come off the reel.)*

END OF PLAY